If you were a

POUND or a

KILOGRAM

by Marcie Aboff

illustrated by Francesca Carabelli

PICTURE WINDOW BOOKS
Minneapolis, Minnesota

Editors: Christianne Jones and Jill Kalz
Designer: Lori Bye
Page Production: Melissa Kes
Art Director: Nathan Gassman
Editorial Director: Nick Healy
The illustrations in this book were created with acrylics.

Picture Window Books
151 Good Counsel Drive
P.O. Box 669
Mankato, MN 56002-0669
877-845-8392
www.picturewindowbooks.com

All books published by Picture Window Books
are manufactured with paper containing
at least 10 percent post-consumer waste.

Library of Congress Cataloging-in-Publication Data
Aboff, Marcie.
If you were a pound or a kilogram / by Marcie Aboff ;
illustrated by Francesca Carabelli.
p. cm. — (Math Fun)
Includes index.
ISBN 978-1-4048-5204-4 (library binding)
ISBN 978-1-4048-5205-1 (paperback)
1. Pound (Unit)—Juvenile literature. 2. Kilogram—
Juvenile literature. 3. Units of measurement—Juvenile
literature. I. Carabelli, Francesca, ill. II. Title.
QC106.A26 2009
530.8'1—dc22   2008037911

Special thanks to our adviser for his expertise:

Stuart Farm, M.Ed., Mathematics Lecturer
University of North Dakota

pound—a unit of English weight measurement
kilogram—a unit of metric weight measurement

If you were a pound
or a kilogram ...

... you could measure the weight of something in **a gym,**

a supermarket,

or a post office.

5

If you were a pound, you would be made up of ounces. There are 16 ounces in 1 pound.

Franklin mixed 16 ounces of sugar and 32 ounces of flour. That makes 1 pound of sugar and 2 pounds of flour.

FLOUR

16 ounces

FLOUR

16 ounces

SUGAR

16 ounces

He added butter and chocolate chips and put the dough in the oven.

He made one giant cookie.

16 ounces = 1 pound

7

If you were a kilogram, you would be made up of grams.
There are 1,000 grams in 1 kilogram.

Ferdie lifts a barbell weighing 2,000 grams.
That's 2 kilograms.

1,000 grams

1,000 grams

1,000 grams = 1 kilogram

Ferdie adds another weight.
Now he lifts 3,000 grams.
That's 3 kilograms.

Ferdie adds one more weight.
Now he lifts 4,000 grams. That's 4 kilograms.

If you were a pound or a kilogram, you could be changed into one another. In fact, 1 pound is about 0.45 kilograms, and 1 kilogram is about 2.2 pounds.

Jimmy surprised Jill with 1 pound of candy. "That's almost half a kilogram of dandy candy!" exclaimed Jill.

Patrick surprised Pearl with 1 kilogram of berries. "That's more than 2 pounds of merry berries!" exclaimed Pearl.

1 pound = about 0.45 kilograms
1 kilogram = about 2.2 pounds

If you were a pound, it would take 2,000 of you to make a ton.

Ezra weighed 4,000 pounds, or 2 tons.
His truck weighed 12,000 pounds, or 6 tons.

If you were a kilogram, it would take 1,000 of you to make a metric ton.

Emo weighed 3,000 kilograms, or 3 metric tons.

His truck weighed 9,000 kilograms, or 9 metric tons.

2,000 pounds = 1 ton
1,000 kilograms = 1 metric ton

If you were a pound or a kilogram, you could be shortened.
The words *pound* and *pounds* can be replaced with the letters *lb*.
The words *kilogram* and *kilograms* can be replaced with the letters *kg*.

This nurse weighs patients in pounds.

PATIENT 1
165 lb
PATIENT 2
132 lb
PATIENT 3
71.5 lb

This nurse weighs patients in kilograms.

PATIENT 1: 75kg
PATIENT 2: 60 kg
PATIENT 3: 325 kg

If you were a pound or a kilogram, you would be found in a supermarket. You would be used to weigh food.

Ducky put some carrots on the scale. They weighed 3 pounds, or about 1.4 kilograms.

3.00

She scooped some barley into a bag and put it on the scale. It weighed 1 pound, or a little less than half a kilogram.

1.00

When Ducky got home, she cooked a delicious soup.

If you were a pound or a kilogram, you would be found at the post office. Your weight would determine how many stamps are needed to mail a package.

Cletus mailed a hay bale to his brother. It weighed 10 pounds, or about 4.5 kilograms.

He mailed corn to his cousin.
It weighed 5 pounds, or about 2.3 kilograms.

He mailed some clover to his aunt.
It weighed one-half of a pound, or
about 0.23 kilograms.

If you were a pound or a kilogram, you would always weigh the same, no matter what you were made of.

Five pounds of popcorn weigh the same as 5 pounds of chocolate.

A 1-kilogram brick weighs the same as
a 1-kilogram bunch of feathers.

You would be "weigh" cool ...

... if you were a pound or a kilogram.

GUESS THE WEIGHT ACTIVITY

What you need:
at least two people
at least 10 items from around the house (for example, a coffee mug,
    a book, a pet's food bowl)
a scale

What you do:
1. Decide on a weight—for example, 2 pounds.
2. Pick one item and ask your friend to guess whether the object weighs
   more or less than the weight you decided on.
3. After he or she answers, weigh the item. If your friend guessed
   correctly, pick another item. If he or she guessed incorrectly, it is
   your turn.
4. Continue until all of the items have been picked. Whoever has the most
   correct answers at the end of the game wins!

Glossary

gram—a unit of metric weight measurement; there are 1,000 grams in 1 kilogram

kilogram—a unit of metric weight measurement (1 kilogram = about 2.2 pounds)

metric ton—a unit of metric weight measurement; there are 1,000 kilograms in 1 metric ton

ounce—a unit of English weight measurement; there are 16 ounces in 1 pound

pound—a unit of English weight measurement (1 pound = about 0.45 kilograms)

ton—a unit of English weight measurement; there are 2,000 pounds in 1 ton

To Learn More

More Books to Read

Kompelien, Tracy. *I Can Measure Weight at Any Rate.* Edina, Minn.: ABDO Pub. Co., 2007.

Schwartz, David M. *Millions to Measure.* New York: HarperCollins, 2003.

On the Web

FactHound offers a safe, fun way to find educator-approved Internet sites related to this book.

Here's what you do:

1. Visit *www.facthound.com*
2. Choose your grade level.
3. Begin your search.

This book's ID number is 9781404852044

Index

Look for all of the books in the Math Fun series:

If You Were a Divided-by Sign
If You Were a Fraction
If You Were a Minus Sign
If You Were a Minute
If You Were a Plus Sign
If You Were a Pound or a Kilogram
If You Were a Quart or a Liter
If You Were a Set
If You Were a Times Sign
If You Were an Even Number
If You Were an Inch or a Centimeter
If You Were an Odd Number